SECRETS AND MYSTERIES OF THE HEART 200 ROUTE

Thomas A. Christie & Julie Christie

Other Books by Thomas A. Christie

Liv Tyler: Star in Ascendance
The Cinema of Richard Linklater
John Hughes and Eighties Cinema
Ferris Bueller's Day Off: The Pocket Movie Guide
The Christmas Movie Book
Notional Identities
The Shadow in the Gallery
The James Bond Movies of the 1980s
Mel Brooks: Genius and Loving It!
The Spectrum of Adventure
A Righteously Awesome Eighties Christmas
Contested Mindscapes
John Hughes FAQ
The Golden Age of Christmas Movies
A Very Spectrum Christmas

Other Books by Thomas A. Christie & Julie Christie

The Heart 200 Book

SECRETS AND MYSTERIES OF THE HEART 200 ROUTE

Thomas A. Christie

&

Julie Christie

Secrets and Mysteries of the Heart 200 Route by Thomas A. Christie and Julie Christie.

First edition published in Great Britain in 2021 by Extremis Publishing Ltd., Suite 218, Castle House, 1 Baker Street, Stirling, FK8 1AL, United Kingdom.
www.extremispublishing.com

Extremis Publishing is a Private Limited Company registered in Scotland (SC509983) whose Registered Office is Suite 218, Castle House, 1 Baker Street, Stirling, FK8 1AL, United Kingdom.

Copyright © Thomas A. Christie and Julie Christie, 2021.

Thomas A. Christie and Julie Christie have asserted the moral right under the Copyright, Designs and Patents Act 1988 to be identified as the authors of this work.

Heart 200 and the Heart 200 Logo are Registered Trademarks, Copyright © Heart 200 Scot Ltd., all rights reserved.

The views expressed in this work are solely those of the authors, and do not necessarily reflect those of the publisher. The publisher hereby disclaims any responsibility for them.

This book is a work of non-fiction. Unless otherwise noted, the authors and the publisher make no explicit guarantees as to the accuracy of the information included in this book and, in some cases, the names of people, places and organisations may have been altered to protect their privacy. All hyperlinks were believed to be live and correctly detailed at the time of publication.

This book may include references to organisations, feature films, television programmes, popular songs, musical bands, novels, reference books, and other creative works, the titles of which are trademarks and/or registered trademarks, and which are the intellectual properties of their respective copyright holders.

All rights reserved. No part of this publication may be reproduced, stored in a retrieval system, or transmitted, in any form or by any means, electronic, mechanical, photocopying, recording or otherwise, without the prior permission in writing of the publisher.

This book is sold subject to the condition that it shall not, by way of trade or otherwise, be lent, re-sold or hired out, or otherwise circulated without the publisher's prior consent in any form of binding or cover other than that in which it is published and without a similar condition including this condition being imposed on the subsequent purchaser.

A CIP catalogue record for this book is available from the British Library.

ISBN: 978-1-7398543-0-0

Typeset in Sorts Mill Goudy, designed by The League of Moveable Type.

Printed and bound in Great Britain by IngramSpark, Chapter House, Pitfield, Kiln Farm, Milton Keynes, MK11 3LW, United Kingdom.

Cover artwork is Copyright © Essevu at Shutterstock Inc.
Frontispiece artwork by Gerhard G. from Pixabay.

Cover design and book design is Copyright © Thomas A. Christie.
Incidental interior vector artwork from Pixabay.

Author images are Copyright © Amy Leitch / Eddy Bryan.

Internal photographic images are Copyright © Thomas A. Christie and Julie Christie, and are sourced from the authors' private collection unless otherwise stated in the Image Credits section, which forms an extension to this legal page.

The copyrights of third parties are reserved. All third party imagery is used under the provision of Fair Use for the purposes of commentary and criticism. While every reasonable effort has been made to contact copyright holders and secure permission for all images reproduced in this work, we offer apologies for any instances in which this was not possible and for any inadvertent omissions.

This book is dedicated to

MR DAVID M. ADDISON

The undisputed maestro of the Scottish road trip

INTRODUCTION

In *The Heart 200 Book*, we explored the many destinations and places of interest to be found along the Heart 200 route—the famous road trip around Stirlingshire and Perthshire, where ancient history, modern attractions and stunning natural scenery meet in a unique travel experience you'll never forget. This time around, however, our objective is a little bit different.

With *Secrets and Mysteries of the Heart 200 Route*, we hope to introduce you to some of the more unusual places and sights in this beautiful area of Scotland: the locations that the tour guides never direct you to, or appealing curiosities that you might otherwise pass by. There are literary links, unexpected historical facts, hidden gems of the area, and a few other surprises too.

The Heart 200 route is a remarkable travel experience, and we would warmly recommend everyone to try their own journey through the area at least once in their life—though ideally, you will want to come back time and again, as no one trip can possibly give you the opportunity to visit everything this road trip has to offer. Each and every destination has something unique to experience, and there is always something new to discover.

For all the latest Heart 200 news, we would like to direct you to the newly-redesigned and relaunched official Heart 200 website at: *www.heart200.scot*. There you will find the most up-to-date information about the route, places of interest, participating companies and organisations, film and TV filming locations, social media links, and much more besides.

Special thanks to our occasional travelling companions Amy Leitch and Eddy Bryan, who shared many of our adventures on the road during our research. Thanks also to everyone who provided images and information for this book, including Cultybraggan Camp, Dr Murray Cook, Auchingarrich Wildlife Centre, Craighead Howfs, the Old Town Jail of Stirling, Simon Howie Ltd., Police Scotland, Old Churches House Hotel, The Fusion Group, Clootie McToot Dumplings, Cairn o' Mohr Winery, Stirling Distillery, Highland Safaris and Perth Treasure Trail.

Don't forget that the Heart 200 mantra is slow tourism; this is exactly the kind of road trip where you will want to take as long as you possibly can to appreciate all of the destinations and discover everything that they have to offer. There are so many things to see and do, it's always best to factor in as much exploring time as you can allow yourself—every place around the route has its own charm and surprises to enjoy.

We hope that you will enjoy reading this book as much as we have enjoyed writing it. As we live and work in the area, we know that there is a great deal about Stirlingshire and Perthshire that deserves being excited about. It is our genuine hope that, once you have read this book, you will want to come and see the Heart 200 route for yourself so that you can find out exactly why this amazing region is considered the very heart of Scotland.

Tom and Julie Christie
October 2021

SECRETS AND MYSTERIES OF THE HEART 200 ROUTE

Thomas A. Christie

&

Julie Christie

# THE BIRNAM OAK

Birnam

It may be synonymous with Shakespeare's 1606 'Scottish Play', *Macbeth*, but the ancient and eye-catching Birnam Oak still stands like a silent sentinel over the village even today. It is known not just by the alternative name of 'Macbeth's Oak', but also in some sources as 'The Hangman's Tree'. Listed by Forestry and Land Scotland as one of the country's most famous oak trees, the Birnam Oak has a trunk measuring five and a half metres wide, while a number of its large spreading branches have been propped up by wooden struts over the years in order to avoid any risk of them collapsing due to their sheer weight.

While the tree has never been dated exactly, experts have estimated that it may be over six hundred years of age—thus meaning that it would already be a well-established tree by Shakespeare's time in the Elizabethan era. It is thought to be the last genuine relic of the Birnam Wood that is mentioned in *Macbeth*; with its enormous height, it is easy to see why the eponymous main character of the play is so troubled by the ghostly prediction that he will only be safe until the day Great Birnam Wood comes to Dunsinane Hill.

The Birnam Oak can be found on the south bank of the River Tay, and—in keeping with Perthshire being popularly known as 'Big Tree Country'—it forms the centrepiece of the celebrated Dunkeld House Tree Trail (*www.dunkeldandbirnam.org.uk/listing/dunkeld-house-tree-trail/*), which celebrates the contribution made to nature conservation by the 'Planting Dukes' of Atholl. Running parallel to the river, the trail covers two thousand years of the area's history, and some truly beautiful natural surroundings along the way.

THE WORDSWORTH CONNECTION

Strathyre

The beautiful village of Strathyre became famous in the Victorian era, when the bustling Strathyre Railway Station (built in 1870)—located at the head of Loch Lubnaig—brought crowds of tourists to visit the beautiful surroundings. These include the sprawling Strathyre Forest and the sight of the thundering River Balvaig nearby. Today the village continues to attract holiday-makers from all over the world—not least on account of its extensive appeal to canoeing, walking and cycling enthusiasts.

Early in the nineteenth century, however, Strathyre was briefly visited by famous literary guests in the form of poet William Wordsworth and his sister Dorothy Wordsworth, who came to visit the area in September 1803. Wordsworth, who—along with Samuel Taylor Coleridge—had published the hugely influential poetical anthology *Lyrical Ballads* in 1798, travelled extensively in this period, often in the company of Dorothy (also an author, poet and diarist, though she had no desire to publish her work).

While the pair enjoyed walks in the scenic hills near the village, it was in Strathyre that Wordsworth is thought to have been inspired to compose his haunting poem 'The Solitary Reaper', later published in 1807 as part of his anthology *Poems, in Two Volumes*. It has since become one of his most instantly-recognisable works, and tells of a young Highland woman harvesting crops as she sings a beautiful refrain. Though set in the Hebrides, with its amazing natural beauty it is easy to see why it was Strathyre which gave Wordsworth the creative motivation to write the poem.

THE GOLDEN TELEPHONE BOX

Dunblane

Visitors to Dunblane in recent years have become used to the sight of the city's famous gold post box, which was gifted its distinctive colour by Royal Mail in 2012 when famous one-time resident and tennis superstar Sir Andy Murray won a Gold Medal in the Men's Singles at the London Olympics. Since then, countless people have had their photos taken at this centrally-located modern landmark... but what is less well-known is the fact that Dunblane has another, entirely different golden visitor attraction to its name.

The golden telephone box in Dunblane, which is situated on an intersection between Old Doune Road and Springfield Terrace, was purchased by the local community as part of British Telecom's 'Adopt a Kiosk' scheme. With mobile phones now ubiquitous throughout society, this project has allowed communities to repurpose public phone boxes for new functions while retaining the visual charm and cultural heritage of their original form, with the Dunblane phone box already becoming a popular destination for sightseers and selfie-hunters.

Painted gold by members of the Dunblane Young Persons Project, the purchase of the telephone box was made possible by the local community council and a donation from the city's nearby wind farm, which has allowed for the creation of a peaceful public space in an otherwise bustling area of the city. Though a fairly recent addition to this ancient place, the telephone box has come to be considered one of Dunblane's quirkiest and most eye-catching curiosities.

PRISONER OF WAR ARTWORK

Cultybraggan, Near Comrie

One of the most amazing places you will encounter on the Heart 200 route, Cultybraggan Camp is a truly unforgettable sight. Situated deep within the heart of beautiful rural Perthshire, the camp's row after row of impressively-preserved metal Nissen huts is today home to a vibrant community of independent businesses and—thanks to the work of Comrie Development Trust (*www.comriedevelopmenttrust.org.uk*), which has painstakingly maintained the site since 2007—also the venue for many different public events throughout the year.

However, the camp wasn't always such an inviting place to visit. Built in 1941, during the Second World War, it was constructed with the aim of housing up to four thousand Prisoners of War from the Axis Powers. These included members of the Nazi *Waffen-SS* ('Armed Protection Squadron'), sailors from U-boats, and *Fallschirmjäger* (paratroopers). Numerous prisoners, such as the late Heinrich Steinmeyer (a one-time member of the *Waffen-SS*, who died in 2014 and whose bequest to Comrie formed the Heinrich Steinmeyer Legacy Fund), spoke regularly of how well they and their fellow countrymen had been treated by the camp authorities during the War.

A museum has been established within the grounds of Cultybraggan Camp to honour its wartime heritage, and among its exhibits are artworks created by Prisoners of War during their period of incarceration which display scenes of their lives during the early-to-mid 1940s. Like the many other fascinating presentations within, these striking images are not to be missed.

THE CONCORDE MUSIC SHOP

Perth

Situated on Perth's bustling Scott Street, the legendary Concorde Music Shop (www.concordemusic.com) was established in 1967 by Norman and Rena Smith and is one of the jewels in the crown of the city's independent business community. The store's main claim to fame is that it is the oldest music shop in Scotland to still be operating under the ownership of the same family that originally founded it, with current owners Garry, Hazel and Craig Smith celebrating fifty years of trading on the 31st of October 2017 to the great interest of the national press.

The Concorde Music Shop is a veritable treasure trove for any music lover, stocking literally thousands of vinyl LPs, singles (both 7" and 12"), picture discs, CDs, and many limited edition items. They also participate in many national music events such as National Album Day, and offer a large range of music-themed accessories and merchandise which include T-shirts, mugs, pictures and even clocks. Originally based in the city's St John's Square, the business moved to its current Scott Street premises in the early 1980s—right at the beginning of the compact disc revolution—and has continued to evolve and diversify in order to satisfy the tastes of their many customers. While an increasing amount of music is now accessed digitally, the Concorde Music Shop is unapologetic in its stalwart support for physical media and has become ever more popular thanks to the recent boom in public interest towards vinyl records. While it has long been a must-visit destination for generations of Perth-based music enthusiasts, it has now become so well-known that people visit from miles around to browse the shop's expansive stock.

THE CONCORDE

concordemusic.com

Music Shop

CHART CD'S — **VINYL** 7" 10"

SECOND HAND VINYL BOUGHT & SOLD

THE OLD WATERMILL

Blair Atholl

The village of Blair Atholl is home to many charming sights, but few as beguiling as its old mill next to the River Tilt. Considered to be Scotland's oldest working watermill, the existing building dates back to around 1830, though historians believe that there had been a mill located on the same site for much longer—from at least the 1590s onwards.

The mill was closed in 1929 and was converted into a shop, but in 1977 the building was extensively renovated and restored by John Ridley with the aid of the last surviving miller's assistant (who, recalling the building's original use from personal memory, was of great help in returning the site to its original glory). By 1993 the old watermill came into the ownership of James and Mary Bruce, and today it is run by their children who operate the building as a very successful tearoom (*www.blairathollwatermill.co.uk*).

Visitors can still see the mill in operation at certain times; the water wheel can only operate when the River Tilt is at full spate, as the correct water level is required for milling. The owners take great pride in the impressive number of products which are produced at the mill, which include wheat, oats, rye and spelt—all stone-ground using traditional techniques. The on-site bakery is home to many products made using flour and oatmeal created at the mill, including cakes, scones, bagels, croissant, bread, and the Blair Atholl Watermill's speciality: their famous carrot cake. These are served in their tea garden and tearoom (based on the location of the building's original grain store), or from their well-stocked shop. In so doing, they keep alive a tradition dating back centuries.

CATHEDRAL BATTLE DAMAGE

Dunkeld

One of the most distinctive sights for miles around, grand Dunkeld Cathedral is a remarkable location. Part working church and part historical ruin—a section of the cathedral's structure is now no longer habitable and is in the care of Historic Environment Scotland—it is home not just to an active worship community (www.dunkeldcathedral.org.uk), but also an extensive museum detailing the building's extensive history throughout the centuries.

Completed in 1501, and constructed upon the site of a monastery dating back even further to sixth or seventh century, the cathedral has a long past and has become the burial place of numerous historical figures—most notably Alexander Stuart, Earl of Buchan, better known as the Wolf of Badenoch. Surrounded by tranquil and well-maintained grounds, it seems difficult to imagine that the cathedral was once at the epicentre of the bloody Battle of Dunkeld on 21 August 1689.

Part of the Jacobite Rising of that same year, the battle took place between Jacobite clans following the recently-deposed King James II and VII and government forces loyal to King William III and II. Government troops occupied the cathedral (as well as the Marquess of Atholl's proximate mansion house) and prepared to defend the area from the advancing Jacobite forces. The fighting was fierce, and the damage caused by the ensuing musket-fire can still be seen embedded in the exterior of the cathedral's walls to this very day. After much bloodshed, the battle eventually ended in a Jacobite withdrawal, but the violent legacy of the conflict remains for all to witness when visiting this unique monument.

THE BROUGH & MacPHERSON SHOP

Comrie

Right at the centre of the town of Comrie lies a striking shop with an extraordinary secret. Based at 1 Dunira Street, in the early twentieth century the building was owned by Messrs. Brough and MacPherson—a well-known draper and ironmonger in the area. When they sought to renovate their premises, however, they were to turn to none other than one of the most acclaimed names in Scottish architecture: Charles Rennie Mackintosh.

The owners commissioned Rennie Mackintosh with precise specifications for the building: the ground floor was to be used as a general store, the first floor as an apartment, and the attic space as workrooms. The renovations took place during the period 1903-04, when Mackintosh was undertaking some of his best work (such as the famous Miss Cranston's tearooms in Glasgow's Sauchiehall Street), which has led to the building in Comrie being of interest to followers of his pioneering designs. Perhaps of greatest note, Mackintosh constructed a tourelle—a small projecting turret—to the corner of the building, which hinted at the influence of Scottish Baronial architecture. In addition to redecorating the shop, flat and attic, Mackintosh also designed the adjacent two-storey office for solicitor John Mitchell.

Though known locally as 'the Brough and MacPherson shop', due to the owners who commissioned the work, the Rennie Mackintosh connection has led to it being informally named 'the Mackintosh Building' by aficionados. Due to its historical significance, the apartment was purchased by the Landmark Trust in 1985, which has since painstakingly restored the original Mackintosh decoration to an exceptional standard.

THE BASTION THIEVES' POT

Stirling

The busy Thistles Shopping Centre at the heart of Stirling has long held a mysterious secret in the form of its shadowy Bastion. Generations of visitors have descended the iron spiral staircase from the shopping mall to discover the remains of the Bastion—now a fascinating mini-museum with interpretation boards explaining how the structure was once part of the city's 16th century Burgh Wall. Once Stirling's dungeon in bygone centuries, the Bastion was extensively remodelled in 2018 with new informational displays and an audio commentary provided by David Kinnaird, the acclaimed 'Happy Hangman' of Stirling Ghost Walks, who has been entertaining audiences with stories of the city's supernatural tales for many years.

While countless guests have visited the Bastion over the years, what is less well known is that beneath the glass-covered floor aperture is the remains of the 'Thieves' Pot', where prisoners would have been condemned to incarceration in ages past. Though this subterranean area is not accessible to the public, Stirling's Burgh Archaeologist—Dr Murray Cook—once explored these dark and cramped environs and discovered that entry could still be gained to its confined interior. The photo opposite was taken by him during his investigation of this restrictive area; a rare image of the claustrophobic place where so many had once been imprisoned and shackled. Between the mediaeval era and the industrial era, small children were sent into the Thieves' Pot with the goal of mining metals from the ground. While such employment of minors is now thankfully long behind us, numerous visitors and workers from adjacent shops still report the ghostly sound of children's voices echoing from the Bastion even today.

KINNOULL HILL TOWER

Perth

If you should be passing Perth's scenic Kinnoull Hill—the perfect viewpoint for some of the most beautiful vistas in all of Perthshire—you may well notice an intriguing ruin perched high upon a nearby crag. If you ask yourself how this striking edifice came to be built in this elevated location, however, you may be surprised to learn that it isn't actually an abandoned ancient structure at all.

Kinnoull Hill Tower is a folly, constructed in the nineteenth century and thought to have been commissioned by the 9th Earl of Kinnoull. The Earl felt that the craggy outcrops along the south side of the hill reminded him of the cliffs along Germany's Rhine Valley, upon which numerous castles have been built, and thus decided that Perth's natural surroundings should be treated to some dramatic grandeur of their own.

While the castellated folly is mainly composed of the eye-catching round tower which dominates the site, the Earl also ordered adjacent ruins to be built including battlements, arches and remnants of walls—all deliberately designed to look as though they are the timeworn relics of a much earlier age. There is even a stone table on the site, which was intended as a picnic area.

The entirety of Kinnoull Hill was donated to Perth in 1924, and in 1991 it became part of a woodland park. This forested country park is a popular destination for walkers , with its many nature trails and stunning views, and the tower is regularly explored by visitors to the area.

THE BISHOP'S PALACE

Dunblane

While the beautiful cathedral is always a popular destination for visitors to Dunblane, its Bishop's Palace is a considerably less widely-recognised attraction. Situated close to the cathedral grounds, the palace is now ruined and its adjacent rectangular well is empty of water. However, when built for Bishop Clement in the mid-thirteenth century the building would have been as grand as its illustrious title suggests.

In its heyday, the palace would have been an expansive and imposing building which would have been in keeping with the public stature of its inhabitant. Its floor space would have been considerably more expansive than its much-depleted current form suggests, with some surveys suggesting that its chambers (now underground) may even once have extended to beneath the main cathedral hall.

Historical records suggest that even as early as 1579, the palace was in a ruined state, and the remnant which exists—behind metal railings, for its protection—is all that is still visible to the public. It is thought that the palace fell into disrepair after the Reformation, with its walls being used as building stone for other construction projects in the area. The four vaulted rooms which can be seen today would once have made up the ground floor of the building's west-facing range, which gives some indication of its original grandeur. Archaeological findings have hinted that there may have been an even earlier structure on the site; a previous palace on the same grounds, now long since lost to history. Nearby interpretation panels offer a visual extrapolation of what the building may once have looked like during its golden age.

THE WORLD'S MOST SCOTTISH SHEEP

Comrie

The amazing Auchingarrich Wildlife Centre (*www.auchingarrich.co.uk*) near Comrie has something for the wildlife enthusiast in all of us. With more than fifty species of animal to discover on-site, as well as fly-fishing ponds, there is always something fun to see and do there. From hatching and handling to pony rides, by way of a tractor circuit, soft play barn and mini-golf, the centre is the perfect destination for anyone with an affinity with the wonderful animal kingdom.

Just when you thought you'd seen everything at Auchingarrich, however, you then discover that they've saved the best for last. Perhaps their best-kept secret, revealed exclusively to us by the centre staff, is the rare Auchingarrich Tartan Sheep—a phenomenon so uncommon that sightings of this remarkable creature have become vanishingly infrequent; the photo opposite has been provided specially by the centre's team.

The tartan sheep was first discovered at Auchingarrich many years ago, and to this day they remain a spectacular sight. When sheared, their wool can be used to make tartan kilts, scarves and blankets. As a lamb, they look similar to a regular sheep, as their colours won't fully develop until they are about one year old. As they get older, their colours can change, so guests who visit more than once may see an entirely new tartan. Tartan sheep are mammals with a lifespan of around 10–12 years, with females (ewes) weighing between 45–100kgs and rams being between 45–160kgs. The tartan sheep mainly feeds on grass, but according to legend they are also said to occasionally enjoy Irn-Bru, Scottish tablet and shortbread.

MARY, QUEEN OF SCOTS' CHAPEL

Kinross

If you happen to be entertaining a guest, hospitality would suggest that you would do anything reasonably possible to make sure that they feel welcome and comfortable. That was certainly the case for the Earl of Douglas, who found himself host to Mary, Queen of Scots—and, some time later, her jailer—at historic Loch Leven Castle near Kinross.

The castle was constructed on Castle Island, on Loch Leven, possibly as early as 1257. It was involved in the Wars of Scottish Independence before being granted to the Douglas family by King Robert II. It remained with the Earls of Douglas for many years, becoming a state prison from the 14th century. While it held numerous noteworthy prisoners, including Robert II himself (prior to taking the crown) and the Archbishop of St Andrews, Patrick Graham, its most famous captive would forever be Mary, Queen of Scots.

Though Mary visited the castle as a guest in 1562 and 1565, when she returned to it in 1567 it was as a prisoner under the custody of Sir William Douglas. Mary had been arrested after the Battle of Carberry Hill and spent most of her time of imprisonment in the Glassin Tower, a sixteenth century addition to the castle on its south-east corner. Mary was ill at the time of her arrival, possibly due to poisoning, and miscarried twins shortly after. Sir William consented to the conversion of a window into a tiny oratory, a private chapel, for Mary's use during her time there. In spite of Douglas's efforts to treat Mary well during her stay, she made numerous escape attempts—including dressing as a washerwoman to evade capture—before finally making her getaway in May 1568 while disguised as a servant. The rest, as they say, is history.

BURNS AND THE BIRKS

Aberfeldy

No visit to the beautiful town of Aberfeldy could possibly be complete without a visit to its famous Birks. The famous 150m high Falls of Moness and eye-catching gorge filled with stately birch trees has become one of the most popular short walks in Scotland, aided by an outstanding waymarked path through the mature mixed woodland.

In 1787, Scotland's national bard Robert Burns visited the Moness gorge for himself (then known as the Dens of Moness), and was so moved by the experience that he wrote a song about the striking natural surroundings. Today, a distinctive monument of four stones each carries a line from the second verse of Burns's song, proclaiming that:

While o'er their heads the hazels hing,
The little birdies blythely sing,
Or lightly flit on wanton wing,
In the birks of Aberfeldy.

Burns's literary connection to the area is also celebrated by information boards and a sculpture of the poet on a wooden bench, drafting the words to his song into a notebook just as he would have done back in the eighteenth century. So famous has Burns's lyrics become, the gorge is now synonymous with the title of his song. The area is now a Site of Special Scientific Interest on account of its flora and fauna, and it is thought that there has been woodland there for as long as eight thousand years.

A LITERARY GIFT TO KENMORE

Kenmore

While Robert Burns's lyrics to *The Birks of Aberfeldy* now feature prominently in the area where he conceived of the song, the great poet was no stranger to Perthshire, having toured the area extensively during his lifetime. One such visit was to the village of Kenmore, where he left a lasting mark of his stay—a poem about the area, etched on the chimney breast of the lounge of the famous Kenmore Hotel (*www.kenmorehotel.com*). It begins:

Admiring Nature in her wildest grace,
These northern scenes with weary feet I trace;
O'er many a winding dale and painful steep,
Th' abodes of covey'd grouse and timid sheep.

The Kenmore Hotel is considered by many to be the oldest hotel in Scotland, having been commissioned in 1572 by Laird Colin Campbell but actually being build upon the site of a tavern which had been there for at least seventy years beforehand. Like many buildings in scenic Kenmore, it retains its historic appearance with a suitably grand front entrance.

Appropriately enough, the hotel lounge where Burns demonstrated his poetic genius is now home to the Poet's Bar. However, Scotland's national bard was not the only famous historical figure to have visited Kenmore Hotel; during the seventeenth century Oliver Cromwell dined there, while Queen Victoria and Prince Albert stayed at the hotel during their honeymoon two hundred years later. The building's staff is still welcoming visitors to Kenmore today.

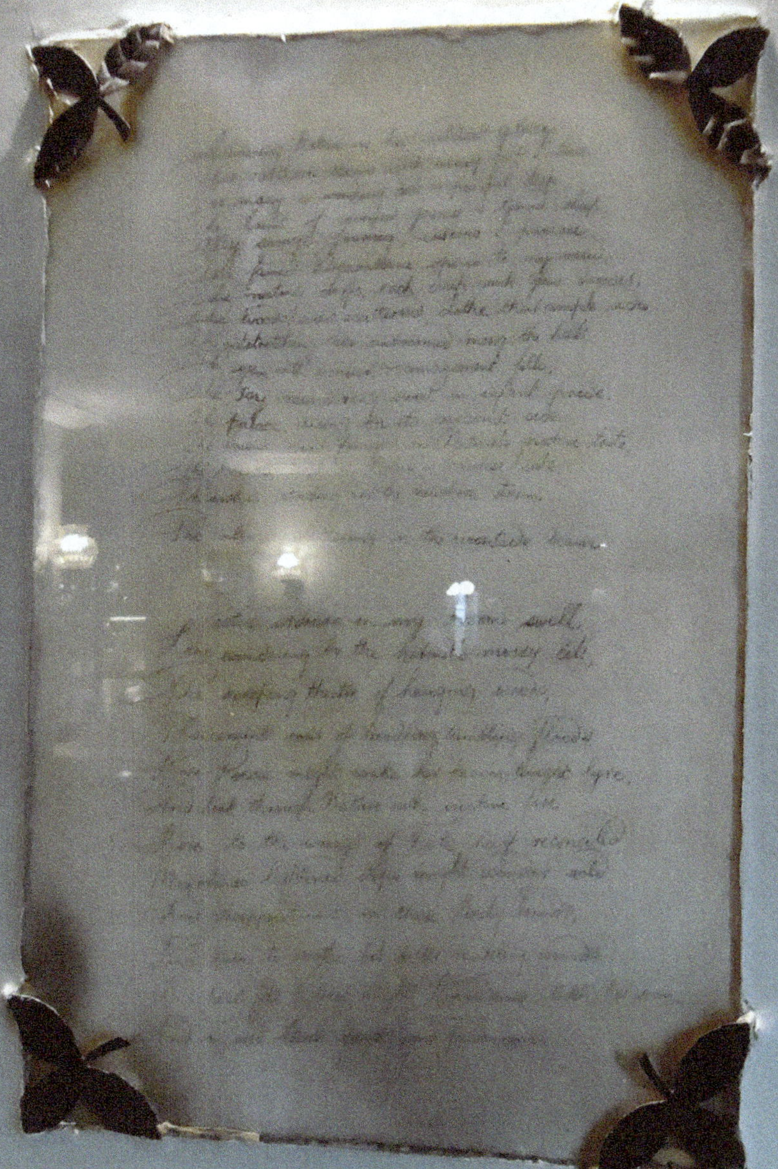

THE BONNETY TREE

Stirling

West of Stirling and just to the south of the village of Cambusbarron lies Gillies Hill, a local landmark where—according to some historical accounts—King Robert the Bruce's followers came running to join the second day of the Battle of Bannockburn in 1314; a development which aided in turning the campaign into a Scottish victory. While some historians in recent years have argued that the camp followers (the Gillies, from which the hill takes its name) had been located elsewhere prior to taking part in the battle, this area of ancient woodland had a special claim to fame due to its legendary Bonnety Tree.

When the Gillies were descending the hill, local legend has it that they had hung their bonnets on the branches of a nearby tree for safety before engaging the English Army. This was thought to be an ancient Scots Pine, which was situated (along with several other trees of the same genus) near Touchadam Craig on the hill's north-west side. As Dr Murray Cook explains in his 2021 book *Bannockburn and Stirling Bridge*, when the nearby Murrayshall Quarry was expanded the Bonnety Tree was felled, and a unique piece of Stirling's story went with it.

However, in 2016 a new Bonnety Tree was planted on the south end of Gillies Hill, thanks to cooperation between conservationists and construction business the Ogilvie Group. The sapling was sourced and transplanted from the area where the original tree had been located, in the hope that one day it would grow to the same stature as its predecessor. It may be some time before the tree reaches a great enough size for people to hang their hats on its branches, but it reflects an important chapter in Scotland's history.

THE LITTLE HOUSES

Dunkeld

Visit historic Dunkeld and you can't possibly miss its remarkable 'Little Houses' leading up to the gate of the cathedral. One of its most famous features, most of these houses were domestic buildings which date from the eighteenth century after the town was badly damaged following the Battle of Dunkeld in 1689. With the Duke of Atholl's support, Dunkeld eventually became a market town, but the eighteenth century merchants' properties eventually became neglected over the years. In 1950, the National Trust spearheaded an ambitious project to restore these buildings in Cathedral Street and around The Cross to their former glory, preserving Dunkeld's cultural heritage for future generations.

Working in collaboration with Perth County Council, the exteriors of the properties were restored sympathetically to reflect their historic character while their interiors were brought up to standard for modern life. Where previous buildings had gone, new houses were constructed to match the style of those surrounding them. Due to this major effort, a total of forty-three buildings were eventually restored—many of them now occupied by busy independent businesses as well as being used as homes.

Today, to walk along Cathedral Street is to personally engage with Dunkeld's long history; plaques are placed on many buildings to explain their significance, including details of the famous people who once lived there in years gone by. The area is still under the auspices of the Little Houses Improvement Scheme, which continues to restore properties and keep Scotland's historic buildings alive.

GREYFRIARS BIODIVERSITY AREA

Perth

You might never expect the level of peace and tranquillity that will greet you right at the heart of the busy city of Perth when arriving at the Greyfriars Biodiversity Area. Created in collaboration between Perth and Kinross Council and Tayside Biodiversity Partnership, this historic graveyard is now a specially-curated natural habitat which many different animals and insects now call home.

While the tall grass may be the first thing you notice upon your arrival, many other types of flora can be found in the area such as meadow buttercup, leopard's bane, cow parsley, lady's mantle and germander speedwell. The information boards located through the grounds give further details of the project, and also explain why biodiversity is so important to our natural environment—especially in large urban areas.

A walk in this area can be serene, with little noise from traffic in the nearby city centre, and it is the perfect place for meditation. On your travels, you might find yourself encountering many different types of creatures including ladybirds, tawny owls, caterpillars, crane flies, swifts, bats, blackbirds, chaffinches, and even Britain's favourite bird, the robin. It really is the ideal location to take a few moments away from the hustle and bustle of everyday life.

The burial ground itself dates back to 1580 and contains many noteworthy gravestones, making it one of the most historically interesting graveyards in all of Scotland. Access to the area is through the north gate in Canal Street or the east gate in Tay Street.

THE HOBBIT HOWFS

Braco

Taking a glance at the photo opposite, you might well think that you were looking at J.R.R. Tolkien's famous Middle-earth… or, at the very least, New Zealand where *The Lord of the Rings* movies were filmed. But in actual fact, this amazing Hobbit-like dwelling can actually be found not in The Shire, but just next to the beautiful village of Braco at the unique Craighead Howfs (*www.craigheadhowf.co.uk*).

Twenty five years ago, Ian and Heather Keir and their young family bought Craighead Farm and began renovating the surrounding buildings and developing the extensive gardens into a diverse horticultural and woodland area—including a wonderful pond that is home to carp and brown trout. They have also added many animals to the farm over the years. In 2006, they opened the Muckle Howf—their first holiday cottage—and have gone on to ever greater success.

Further additions to the farm have been made in the form of the Wee Howf, Summer Howf and Tree Howf, but what has arguably captured the public imagination even more in recent years has been the arrival of the Hobbit Howfs—named, appropriately enough, 'The Burrow' and 'Bag End'. Just like the underground homes described by Tolkien in his fantasy novels, these Hobbit Howfs are cosy and inviting, and supplied with everything you could want for a peaceful holiday away from the busy world outside. The furniture and fittings are all very much in keeping with the diminutive creatures popularised in *The Hobbit* books and films, though thankfully full-sized so that human beings can use them easily! A trip to the Hobbit Howfs really will take you into another world; one that you will never forget.

THE EARTHQUAKE HOUSE

Comrie

Take a trip to the western edge of Comrie and you will find an innocuous-looking building in a field near The Ross. It may seem a little out of place, until you realise that not only has it been standing there since 1874 but that it has been fulfilling an important task ever since. The building is known as the Earthquake House, and it is situated directly above the Highland Boundary Fault—the very geographical feature that gives Comrie its distinctive nickname of 'The Shaky Toun'.

Comrie is the most seismically active town in Britain, having experienced more earth tremors than anywhere else in the country. Its first earthquake was recorded back in 1597, and seismic activity continued in the area—most notably the great earthquake of 1839. This persuaded the townspeople to establish a pioneering seismometer in Comrie in 1840 to track tectonic activity, but a further series of quakes in 1869 heightened scientific interest and brought about the construction of the Earthquake House that we see today; the world's first purpose-built observation centre for earthquake detection.

While the building fell out of use in 1911, it would remain undamaged and eventually became classified as a building of special historical or architectural interest in 1977. It was thus one of the country's smallest listed buildings. However, some years later in 1988 the building was once again restored to its original function when the British Geographical Survey installed new seismographic recording equipment, and it remains in place today—still detecting tremors on the bedrock where it was constructed all those years ago.

THE OLD TOWN JAIL

Stirling

Stirling's Old Town Jail (*www.oldtownjail.co.uk*) first opened in 1847 under the name of the New County Jail. The final Reformed Prison to be constructed in Victorian Scotland, its opening coincided with the closure of the nearby jail at the Tolbooth. Its initial purpose was to rehabilitate prisoners through training and education, though it eventually transitioned from being a civilian prison to a military detention barracks between 1888 and 1935.

The cells, designed by architect Thomas Brown, reflected William Brebner's aim of using the separation of inmates as a tool of their rehabilitation—encouraging solitary reflection and study while isolating them from the 'bad influence' of other prisoners. The jail has fifty-one cells (or fifty-seven, if store rooms were adapted to house inmates), spread over five floors on two wings extending east and west from a central tower. All of the cell windows are south-facing, while every cell could be seen from one location—the panopticon—on the first floor, which faces the central tower. The only time prisoners would be permitted out of their cells would be for their half-hour daily exercise period on one of the two roof walkways.

Today, you can see these historic cells for yourself—and in more pleasant circumstances than their original inhabitants! Stirling Old Town Jail is a multiple award-winning visitor attraction, rated highly by the public and the winner of the TripAdvisor Travellers' Choice Award. They offer guided tours and, with the aid of audio equipment, self-guided tours which explore what prison life was like in the past—giving an insight not just into local stories of criminal acts and their punishment, but also the effects of prison reform over the decades.

THE FIRST HAGGIS IN SPACE

Dunning

Scotland is no stranger to world firsts—it is, after all, the country whose pioneering inhabitants brought the world the telephone, television, penicillin, refrigerator, ATM, vacuum flask, and even the humble toaster. But in 2021 Scotland was to bear witness to an entirely new record-breaking feat when a popular Perthshire-based firm of butchers, Simon Howie Ltd. (*www.thescottishbutcher.com*), launched a haggis into space for the first time.

In an out-of-this-world achievement, the company joined forces with Scotland's acclaimed launch provider Stratonauts to propel their best-selling Original Haggis into orbit (and return it safely to Earth again). One of the country's most well-known national dishes, haggis was first mentioned way back in 1430, and every January since 1801 it is consumed at Burns Suppers across the world in honour of Robert Burns's oft-quoted 1787 poem, *Address to a Haggis*. But our beloved national bard could scarcely have imagined that his favoured repast would one day be rocketing off where no haggis had gone before!

In 2010, Simon Howie Ltd. had hosted the world's highest Burns Supper on the summit of Mount Kilimanjaro, but eleven years later the company's ambitions were even more grand. Launching from the firm's headquarters in Dunning, the haggis flew over twenty miles (107.293 feet) above the Earth's surface—four times the height of Mount Everest. During its journey, it travelled more than 85km with a flight lasting two hours and thirty-seven minutes, passing over Stirling, Falkirk, Edinburgh and the Pentland Hills before safely touching down in Lauder. The haggis has since been safely preserved at the Dunning HQ for posterity.

THE FORTINGALL BELL

Fortingall

A village known for many attractions, Fortingall immediately calls to mind its famous ancient yew tree, its stone circles, or its prominent and highly-rated Arts and Crafts-style hotel. However, until recently Fortingall was also home to a rare artefact of historical significance: the Fortingall Bell.

Fortingall has been linked to the dawn of Scottish Christianity for many centuries—its very name derives from the Gaelic *Fartairchill*, meaning 'escarpment church'. Its Parish Church is located on ground thought to be the site of a daughter monastery founded around 700AD from the Island of Iona by its Bishop, Coeddi.

Dating back to this time was a distinctive Celtic quadrangular hand-bell made from iron and coated with bronze. It is believed to have been in the possession of the Fortingall Church for over 1200 years, and in latter years was situated in a locked cage within a special niche behind the pulpit which was designed to keep it safe yet available for the public to view. The reason for the bell's significance (apart from its great age) is that it may once have belonged to St Adamnán of Iona, and is an excellent example of the type of bell common in Ireland and used by early missionaries of the Columban Church.

Tragically, the bell was stolen from the church in September 2017, and at time of writing has not been recovered. Given its incalculable value to the church's history, Police Scotland are still investigating this egregious theft, and retain hope that one day the bell may yet be recovered and returned to its rightful home for everyone to view once more.

THE FAIR MAID'S STATUE

Perth

Of all Sir Walter Scott's acclaimed historical novels, none are quite so beloved in the city of Perth as his 1828 book *The Fair Maid of Perth*. Based in Perth and other areas of Scotland, the novel is based around the year 1396 at the time of the Battle of the North Inch (or 'Battle of the Clans') where King Robert III staged a battle between the Clan Chattan and Clan Quhele on what is now the North Inch park. One of the *Waverley* novels, its plot centres around the eponymous Fair Maid—Catherine Glover, daughter of city glove-maker Simon Glover, who eventually finds herself embroiled in the intrigues of the King's court.

The story, with its fictionalised plot weaving around real historical events, was popular in its day and eventually came to be adapted by composer Georges Bizet as a four-act opera, *La jolie fille de Perth*, in 1867. It would later be adapted into two silent films, the first directed by Eliot Stannard in 1923 and the second helmed by Miles Mander in 1926. But it is Scott's original novel which continues to be honoured in Perth, as the city took its story to its heart and celebrates its to this day.

Perhaps the most obvious exponent of Perth's affection for the character of Catherine Glover comes in the form of an eye-catching bronze statue of the Fair Maid which was created in 1995 by sculptor Graham Ibbeson. The statue can be found on the city's high street, seated on a bench with a bound book placed on her lap. Catherine is dressed in period-accurate medieval clothing and is staring into the distance as though waiting for someone. Just how many tales will she have heard from visitors and passers-by over the years?

THE OLDEST HOUSE IN PERTH

Perth

It is thought that Sir Walter Scott drew inspiration for the events of *The Fair Maid of Perth* from what is now known as 'The Fair Maid's House'—a Category B listed building based in North Port near Perth city centre. Dating as far back as 1475 (almost eighty years after the events of the novel), though heavily renovated and extended in 1629, the two-storey house's connection to Scott's work comes from the fact that it was used for more than a century and a half by the Glover Incorporation of Perth as their meeting hall: their motto, 'Grace and Peace', can still be seen above the building's main doorway.

The house is thought to be the oldest secular building in Perth, and is highly distinctive with its stair tower. Its masonry has been renewed over the years, whilst its interior was redesigned by architects J. & G. Young in 1893–94 at the request of the building's owner, solicitor William Japp. There is further evidence of the building's ancient origins in that its north wall was once part of the long-since-demolished Blackfriars Monastery (disestablished in 1569), while a fireplace and prayer niche on the first floor are thought to date back to the house's fifteenth century origins.

Between 2010–11, the building was restored and extended by architectural firm Page\Park Architects for the Royal Scottish Geographical Society—painstaking work which won a commendation at the Scottish Civic Trust Awards. The building is now a visitor and education centre where guests can discover more about geography and the physical sciences, cartography, famous explorers, and many other fascinating facts besides.

THE STIRLING TRACT ENTERPRISE

Stirling

Today, the grand Viewforth building is the headquarters of Stirling Council... but it was not always so. Back in the Victorian era, the property was the home of Peter Drummond—a wealthy seed merchant, and the founder of the Stirling Tract Enterprise. It was due to the efforts of the Drummond family that Stirling became one of Scotland's most prominent publishing towns. The Stirling Tract Enterprise was opened in 1848, and with humble beginnings: the first publications were sold from a little box at the company's seed premises, Messrs Drummond and Sons, in King Street. By 1852, Peter Drummond had committed himself to full-time publishing efforts. His ambitions were rewarded, as by 1872 an estimated 60 million tracts had been circulated by the company. The Stirling Tract Enterprise continued to grow rapidly, and by the time it relocated to newly-built premises in Dumbarton Road in 1888 it had earned a reputation as a genuinely global publishing business.

At the height of its popularity, it is often noted that an extra track had to be added to Stirling Railway Station just to cope with the demand for the company's publications, which were shipped all over the world to overseas markets. Though their publicational efforts had started with tracts (short pamphlets/leaflets), as the business grew its output diversified into magazines and books. Their releases continued to be popular throughout both World Wars, but as the twentieth century continued the business gradually went into decline. The company eventually moved to more compact premises in Murray Place before eventually closing in 1980. But Viewforth remains one of Stirling's most prominent buildings, and a reminder of its proud publishing history.

THE SECRET CHAPEL

Dunblane

Nobody who visits beautiful Dunblane can be in any doubt of its long and well-preserved religious history, but sometimes even this most prominent of Scottish cathedral cities can present the world with an amazing surprise from the past.

Located at the Old Churches House Hotel, the Secret Chapel is an amazing glimpse into Scotland's past. This thirteenth century chapel was uncovered during renovation work in 1961, when a team of volunteers were converting a row of cottages into a meeting place and ecumenical respite centre. Clearing through centuries of mud and detritus, the volunteers were amazed at the condition of the building's interior, and subsequent research indicated that it had once been a place of worship—a theory which was reinforced when a body was found buried beneath the table altar in an east-west position in line with early Christian ceremonial burial. Other discoveries included a small well which may have been used in communion ceremonies and cupboards once thought to have housed communion vessels. A wooden cross was erected on the platform outside.

As the years passed, Scottish Churches House eventually became Old Churches House Hotel (www.oldchurcheshouse.com), and the new owners spent two years intensively restoring the chapel to its former glory. It now features newly-fitted seating, lighting, and a font which was relocated from a church in Selkirk. Once their efforts were complete, it was opened to the public and remains so at time of writing. As well as being a popular visitor attraction, the chapel is also used for weddings, christenings and blessings—just as it would have been in ages past.

THE HIGHLAND DROVERS MUSEUM

Crieff

The busy Crieff Visitor Centre, with its restaurant area and well-stocked shop, is always a popular venue for people coming to the town. But what is less known is that the centre contains a remarkable hidden gem in the form of its Highland Drovers Museum, which can be accessed from a passageway at the back of the shopping area.

Complete with informational boards and various artefacts, the compact museum is a treasure trove of facts about the Highland Drovers—the hardy figures from Scotland's past who braved harsh terrain, an unforgiving climate and even the machinations of rustlers in order to deliver their cattle from the Highlands to the famous market in Crieff. From there, they would often drive the animals from Scotland to the south of England, to regions such as East Anglia and even London.

The exhibition brings to life the Great Tryst in Crieff, which existed throughout the eighteenth and nineteenth centuries, and explains not just the hardships which faced the Highland Drovers during their unforgiving duties but also the reasons why the droving tradition eventually came to an end. Visitors are also introduced to historical characters such as Rob Roy MacGregor, and will learn the connection they had to the age of droving.

Scotland's significant livestock traditions are often unfairly overlooked, which makes exhibitions such as this one all the more important. It helps not just to bring the past to life, but also to explain just why Crieff played such a vital part in Scotland's society and economy.

CLOOTIE McTOOT DUMPLINGS

Abernethy, Near Perth

Scotland has many culinary traditions, and one of them is brought to life in high style at Clootie McToot Dumplings (*www.clootiemctootdumplings.com*). Based in the scenic village of Abernethy, the company celebrates the traditional Scottish clootie dumpling—delicious Scottish fruit puddings cooked by a unique method—in more ways than you ever thought possible. Established by Michelle Maddox in 2017, Clootie McToot Dumplings creates a range of traditional clootie dumplings—prepared individually with the best and freshest of ingredients using a recipe that has been handed down through generations. Some feature a modern twist or two to the original recipe, but all are delicious when served warm with ice cream or a dash of hot custard. Over time, the company has diversified widely and now also offers clootie dumpling kits, a Harris Tweed collection, clothing and jewellery, wedding gifts and favours, and even a popular children's book written by Michelle Maddox herself and beautifully illustrated by Jimmy Glen. The company's speciality dumplings are presented beautifully in a variety of different styles, and new products are continually being added to the range.

The first recipe for a clootie dumpling dates back to the mid-eighteenth century, and Clootie McToot Dumplings do an admirable job in not just retaining the dish's proud heritage but bringing it right into the present day. They use freshly-boiled cloots (not pillowcases, as was the case in Scotland's past!), and offer a range of Sterling silver charms to commemorate the old tradition of mixing a lucky charm into the dumpling before boiling it. The company offers workshops for visitors, and regularly attends farmer' markets and game fairs all across Scotland.

STEVENSON IN PITLOCHRY

Pitlochry

One of Victorian Scotland's most beloved novelists and essayists, Robert Louis Stevenson enchanted and fascinated the nation with books such as *Treasure Island*, *Kidnapped*, and *The Strange Case of Dr Jekyll and Mr Hyde*. What is less widely known, however, is his connection to the Heart 200 route due to his time in the beautiful town of Pitlochry.

While Stevenson's name may be more immediately connected to Edinburgh or even Samoa, where he settled later in his life, he visited Pitlochry in June 1881 while on holiday with his wife Frances and mother Margaret, staying at the town's celebrated Fisher Hotel. The group later moved on to Kinnaird Cottage in nearby Moulin, eventually leaving for Braemar on the 1st of August.

A famously prolific author, during his short time in Pitlochry he was working industriously on the manuscripts which would eventually become the novels *Thrawn Janet* (1881), *The Merry Men* (1882), and *The Body Snatcher* (1884). Stevenson was clearly struck by the beauty of the surrounding area; he wrote approvingly of scenic Perthshire to friends during his time there.

During this period, Stevenson visited many areas which are now located on the Heart 200 route; he came to Blair Atholl on 22nd August 1880 when heading north to holiday in Strathpeffer, while he and his father—lighthouse engineer Thomas Stevenson—spent time together exploring Lochearnhead in June 1882. Stevenson and his family also stayed in Bridge of Allan between 14th June and 6th July 1859, and visited Perth in the July of 1859.

THE SPECTRAL WATER HORSE

Lochearnhead

Scotland has no shortage of mystical legends to its name, from the Loch Ness Monster all the way through to the Nine Maidens of Dundee and the Ghost Piper of Clanyard Bay. But one of the most remarkable supernatural stories of the Heart 200 route took place in none other than the scenic village of Lochearnhead.

Loch Earn is today a popular destination for water sports enthusiasts, but in times gone by—according to local legend—it was home to an *each-uisge*: a water spirit in the form of a horse. This paranormal entity was said to have been driven out of nearby Loch Tay by Fingal (himself a giant of legend) and chased across the hills to its new home in Loch Earn.

Unlike the comparatively passive kelpie, an *each-uisge* is a dangerous creature indeed. It can shift its shape into other forms such as a conventional horse... or even a human being. Take care if you should be enticed to ride on the horse's back, however; legend has it that the rider's hands will become stuck fast to the neck of the *each-uisge* as it dives deep into the loch, making it impossible to escape. The hapless rider will drown in the deep water, with their body quickly being devoured by the spirit—with the singular exception of their liver, which is said to return to the loch's surface as a warning to any who would trifle with the spectral water horse.

It is thought that the legend has its origins in the strong currents which run through Loch Earn, which have claimed the lives of inexperienced swimmers over the ages. It is a timely reminder to always treat the water with respect, and to never forget the depth of Scotland's lochs.

THE DEIL'S CAULDRON

Comrie

Only a short walk from Comrie lies the Deil's Cauldron, sometimes known as the Falls of Lednock. A few miles to the west of the town, it is a popular destination for a circular walk that lasts a few hours, and provides an eye-popping view of some truly amazing natural beauty. However, this attractive tree-lined amphitheatre is more than just a treat for sightseers, as it is also the location of an intriguing local legend.

With the thundering torrent of the River Lednock crashing down into frothing rapids, you may well think that the fast-moving water itself is the source of its devilish epithet given their resemblance to a bubbling cauldron. But in actual fact, the waterfall was once said to be the home of a malevolent 'brownie', or water elf, which was named *Uris-chidh*. Not being particularly fond of visitors, this antagonistic imp sought to trick passers-by into plunging to their death in the churning cauldron of deep water. The legend does suggest that *Uris-chidh* eventually received his just desserts, however. According to the story, the elf grew cold one winter and came to Comrie in disguise. He came to a cottage owned by an elderly woman, who recognised his true form and invited him to sit by the fire. She then threw embers from her fireplace over the brownie, exorcising him, and he was never seen or heard from again.

Thankfully for visitors seeking to avoid the machinations of *Uris-chidh*, today there are conveniently-placed observation platforms to allow people to view the majesty of the waterfall for themselves—without having to get too close to the broiling crucible of foaming water below!

THE OUTLANDER EFFECT

Stirling

There's no denying the massive success enjoyed by *Outlander*, Diana Gabaldon's series of historical drama novels, or its television adaptation which is avidly followed by huge audiences all over the world. First screened on the Starz Network in 2014, the TV series continues to attract new fans with every passing year. Filming in locations all across Scotland, scenes have been shot in areas along the Heart 200 route over the years, but perhaps one of the most surprising destinations has been the famously picturesque campus of Stirling University.

In *Outlander*'s season two, Stirling University's Pathfoot Building—built in 1967—was used as the location of 'Inverness College'; its trademark exterior steps are immediately recognisable on the show. The same building's Crush Hall is also visible in some interior shots. The Pathfoot Building was the first to be completed when the University's campus opened to students, and is now a listed building. Since then, countless undergraduates and postgraduates have studied within its halls, attending lectures, tutorials, and supervision meetings. It is also a public art space, being home to the University's public art collection. In the years that followed, many new buildings have been added to the campus, and the largest of them is the centrally-situated Cottrell Building—named for the University's first principal, Frank Cottrell. The Cottrell Building is connected to the Andrew Miller Building (home of the University Library) by means of a transparent flyover walkway to the Atrium, and this distinctive corridor was used in season four of *Outlander*... as a debarkation walkway at Boston Airport! So a visit to the University is always highly recommended—in any time period.

MOIRLANICH LONGHOUSE

Killin

Just a short distance from the picturesque village of Killin, there is an historical attraction where time literally stands still. The Moirlanich Longhouse is a painstakingly conserved cottage which gives visitors a remarkable insight into what life would have been like in a Scottish rural area during the nineteenth century.

Now in the care of the National Trust for Scotland, the Moirlanich Longhouse preserves a long-bygone way of life; the cruck-framed byre was once a family home, and its interior has remained largely unchanged since its last inhabitant left the building back in 1968. Visitors can view the family living area (separated by a wooden partition from the cattle byre) and see the fixtures and fittings of an authentic home of this era which include box beds, a Scotch dresser, original wallpaper, and a 'hingin' lum'—a hanging chimney which used the wall for support and was placed over an open stone hearth like a canopy to channel fumes out of the building.

While the cattle byre was once home to three milking cows, today it is instead used to display the farming tools that would have been used in the building's agricultural past. The thatch used to originally roof the building can still be seen under its current tin covering. There is also a tool shed which is now full of exhibits from the house, including its inhabitants' clothing (discovered in its roof space), along with photographs chronicling a community that has now been lost to time. A visit to this astonishingly well-maintained location is highly recommended for anyone with an interest in Scottish cultural history.

A VIGILANT LION

Callander

Like so many places throughout Scotland, the bustling town of Callander has a centrally-located war memorial in tribute to the many brave people of the community who laid down their lives in the defence of their country during the World Wars. Situated on Ancaster Square, the impressive freestanding obelisk of the Callander war memorial was designed in the style of a traditional Scottish mercat cross, with its 35-foot-high stone column used regularly as the focal point for Services of Remembrance to ensure that, as the inscription appropriately puts it, 'their names liveth for evermore' and their ultimate sacrifice will never be forgotten.

In 1919, following the conclusion of the Great War, Callander District War Memorial Committee was founded to oversee the construction of a memorial designed by Archibald Kay and built by architect Alastair McMichael. It was officially unveiled in 1921 by the Earl of Ancaster, with 66 names of the honoured fallen inscribed across three separate bronze plaques. Following World War II, a further 13 residents' names were added to the monument.

However, the Callander war memorial also holds an enigmatic secret. At its summit is a heraldic lion rampant clutching a shield—one of the most ancient symbols of Scotland. According to local legend, when the memorial was erected the lion's head was positioned very deliberately so that it could always keep one eye on the clock tower of St Kessog's Church (situated directly across the road) and the other on the bar door of the famous Ancaster Arms Hotel nearby. A deliberately tongue-in-cheek design choice, or simply an urban myth? One thing is for sure: the sharp-eyed lion isn't giving up its mysteries to anyone.

THE MONKEY PUZZLE TREE

Aberfeldy

Born in Weem, near Aberfeldy, Archibald Menzies was a surgeon, explorer, botanist and naturalist whose career was widely admired in his day. He remains widely honoured today for his contribution to research. During his work with the Royal Botanic Gardens, he was encouraged by John Hope—a professor of botany at Edinburgh University—to pursue a a career in medicine. Menzies did just that, and after qualifying as a surgeon he joined the Royal Navy. In the process, he not only travelled around the world but also made some fascinating discoveries.

Menzies had a fascinating career spanning many voyages, and his name has been immortalised in several plants that he discovered during his lifetime. However, he is perhaps best remembered in popular culture for his role in bringing the Chile Pine tree, or *Araucaria araucana*, to Britain for the first time. In 1795 he nurtured some seeds from Chile on the voyage home to the United Kingdom, eventually raising five healthy specimens by the time he returned to port. The 'Monkey Puzzle Tree', as it came to be known, eventually became a popular fixture in nineteenth century formal gardens across the country. The tree's eccentric name has been traced back to English barrister Charles Austin who, upon seeing it for the first time, made the comment that it 'would puzzle a monkey to climb that'. As the tree did not have a popular name at that point in time, Austin's observation eventually came to form the term by which it is still known. Today, the Monkey Puzzle Tree is endangered in its native Chile, but specimens of the tree can still be seen at stately Castle Menzies in Perthshire, where Archibald Menzies started his career in horticulture all those years ago.

CAIRN O' MOHR

Perth

Nestled in the beautiful rolling fields of the Carse of Gowrie near Perth is a unique winery by the name of Cairn o' Mohr (*www.cairnomohr.com*). Established in 1987 by Ron and Judith Gillies in Errol, this fruit wine and cider company has been serving the public with award-winning country wines for decades—and continues to diversify its output with new brands even now. The owners strongly believe in sourcing ingredients locally, and given Perthshire's worldwide reputation for soft fruits there's no doubting the superb quality of the products on offer. Following the company's foundation, a core range of five types of wine were established: strawberry, raspberry, bramble, elderberry and oak leaf. Other flavours were added, ranging from sparkling oak and elder to sparkling strawberry, and this led to various limited editions including Clever Current, Shrubbery, Berry Up, Mulled Elderberry and Berry Christmas. Bottled ciders, Pictish draft ciders and non-alcoholic beverages followed, and the premises were augmented by a popular bar and bistro, the Pickled Peacock, in 2010.

One of Perthshire's true gems, Cairn o' Mohr also operates a wine club, offers guided tours, and are still experimenting with exciting new flavours for their customers. Their popular goods are sold by stockists as far away as the Highlands, Belfast and London. However, this description cannot come close to explaining just what a distinctive place Cairn o' Mohr actually is; with its extraordinary exterior decoration (don't miss their famous giant carved heads) and eccentricities bordering on genius, it's the kind of location you really have to experience for yourself. So why not do just that? The warmest of welcomes will await you there.

THE TALE OF RED CAP

Stirling

Distilled, bottled and labelled in the shadow of Stirling Castle, the products of Stirling Distillery (*www.stirlingdistillery.co.uk*) come from the city's first legal distillery on the Castle Rock. Especially renowned for their London Dry Gin, made with foraged Stirlingshire nettles, the company's gins range from the classic to the eclectic—celebrating local history and folklore. Their gin liqueurs are part of their Folklore Collection, inspired by the mythology of Stirling. But few are quite so mysterious as the enigmatic tale of Red Cap—now immortalised in the form of a popular raspberry gin liqueur.

So the story goes, centuries ago a farmer named David Rae, who hailed from nearby Tullibody, fell in love with a local woman called Janet Cokley and married her. However, the union was not a happy one, as Janet was rather flirtatious and vain which led to her gaining a reputation in the village. Some time later, David met a fairy—who went by the name of 'Red Cap'—and confided in him his marital woes. Red Cap suggested that David place a magic stone in Janet's broth to change her ways, but to his dismay she discovered it and promptly threw it away.

On Halloween night, David met Red Cap again and explained that the scheme had not gone to plan. The fairy then promised that if Janet did not change her ways in the coming year, he and his fellow sprites would whisk her away. Janet continued to be ostracised in her community over the coming year, and the following Halloween David persuaded her to have an early night. Sure enough, Janet disappeared and was never seen again… but locals claimed to have seen her on a cloud, being borne away to Dumyat Hill and from there on to the Fairy Knowe.

ST ADAMNAN'S CROSS

Dull, Near Aberfeldy

St Adamnán (sometimes called 'Eunan') was an abbot at Iona Abbey who travelled widely throughout Scotland and England as he spread the word of the Christian faith. He maintained a friendship with Northumbria's King Aldfrith, and made many trips to the mainland to teach about the Gospel. As a canon jurist and hagiographer, he wrote a number of significant texts including *The Life of Columba*—now considered one of the most important works to have been written in early medieval Scotland.

In the seventh century, local tradition has it that Adamnán came to the Glen Lyon area to continue his evangelical work and reportedly became very fond of the area. Christianity eventually superseded the pagan religions common to the region at the time, and it is thought by many historians that the present-day Fortingall Parish Church is located on the site of a monastery which was established by missionaries from Iona.

So great was Adamnán's admiration for the region, some local legends suggest that prior to his death in 704AD he was asked where he would like to be buried, and he requested that his body be carried from the glen on a wooden dul, or bearer. Wherever the dul broke, that was to be his burial spot. Sure enough, it split in two at the site of what is now the village of Dull, near Aberfeldy—and, years later, home of the acclaimed Highland Safaris (www.highlandsafaris.net). Some accounts have suggested that a monastery was built where the current standing stone is situated, but that it was so successful it was eventually moved to St Andrews. Meanwhile, the relics of St Adamnán were taken to Ireland in 724 before returning to Iona in 730.

THE MELVILLE MONUMENT

Comrie

At 22 metres (72 feet) high, the towering Melville Monument is one of the most distinctive landmarks in Comrie. Situated at a prominent position overlooking the town, it has become a popular destination for walks (albeit rather strenuous ones, given the steep incline leading up to its position on the craggy, 256m-high Dun More). The imposing granite obelisk was commissioned in memory of the first Viscount Melville, Henry Dundas—Chief Minister of Scotland under William Pitt the Younger. It was designed by James Gillespie Graham and built in 1812, just a year after the death of Dundas.

As Scotland's most powerful politician of the late eighteenth century, his memory was enshrined in a number of statues and monuments after his death—most notably the Edinburgh Melville Monument, which is modelled on Trajan's Column and is located in St Andrew Square. Today, however, Henry Dundas has become a controversial figure due to his opposition to abolishing slavery; in 1792 he had an amendment inserted into William Wilberforce's parliamentary bill which saw the British slave trade continue to be legal for a further fifteen years, and this has led to calls for the monument to carry an additional plaque which details Dundas's role in prolonging slavery's legal status in Britain.

One of the most unexpected facts about the monument in Comrie is that, being so high, it was struck by lightning in 1894 and had to be repaired. When a steeplejack was called in to ensure the obelisk was restored safely, he discovered on ascending to its pinnacle that he could see all the way to Arthur's Seat in Edinburgh—more than sixty miles away!

THE MEIKLEOUR BEECH HEDGE

Blairgowrie

Just south of Blairgowrie and Rattray, on the A93 Perth-Blairgowrie road, lies an incredible sight indeed: the lofty Meikleour Beech Hedge, which from 1966 has been recognised by the Guinness Book of Records as the highest hedge in the world—and also, incidentally, the longest hedge in Britain. It is approximately 530m long (about a third of a mile), and measures 30m high (approx. 100ft).

The hedge was planted back in 1745 by Jean Mercer and Robert Murray Nairne on the Meikleour Estate. The workers who were employed to plant the European Beech (*Fagus sylvatica*) were called away to serve during the Jacobite Rebellion of that same year, and all were killed (including Nairne himself) when fighting at the Battle of Culloden. It was thus decided that the hedge would be allowed to grow up towards the heavens in memory of the men who had died when it was planted.

Due to its location, the hedge can be viewed all year round. In the winter, it takes on a brown appearance and thins dramatically until new growth appears in the springtime. General practice is for the hedge to be trimmed every decade, though at time of writing its most recent trim in 2019 was actually the first for nearly twenty years. This painstaking work is undertaken by the Meikleour Trust, with the process taking around six weeks (with the average team comprising four workers, making use of hand-held equipment and a hydraulic lift). It remains one of the most remarkable sights in Scottish forestry, and remains a landmark that is dear to the heart of many people in the Blairgowrie area.

THE GHOSTS OF KILLIECRANKIE

Killiecrankie

The beautiful village of Killiecrankie is today a favoured destination for watersports enthusiasts, walkers and anyone who loves the great outdoors. Nestled near the River Garry, it is the perfect place for nature lovers, picnics, or anyone who is simply seeking a bit of solitude from life's frantic pace. However, this serene place was not always quite so peaceful.

In July 1689, this was the location of the bloody Battle of Killiecrankie, a clash of the first Jacobite Rising where thousands of government soldiers and two troops of cavalry—under the command of Hugh Mackay of Scourie—were rushing to recapture Blair Castle, which had been taken by Jacobite Highlanders under Patrick Stewart of Ballechin. Standing the way of these soldiers was a smaller but dedicated group of Highlanders led by James Graham of Claverhouse. The Jacobites chose their moment, holding off their assault until just after sunset and then charging the government troops on unforgiving terrain. Mackay's forces attempted to retreat but, trapped against the gorge, found that they had no route of escape. The result was a victory for the Highlanders, though at great cost—James Graham was mortally wounded.

The scale of the massacre has certainly left its mark on history; numerous people in more recent times have claimed to see spectral apparitions of soldiers from both sides lying wounded on the battlefield, as though their suffering was eerily frozen in time. One account from the early years of the twentieth century suggested not just the presence of retreating troops and slaughtered bodies, but also of a mysterious ghostly young girl looting corpses. So if you should happen to be visiting the area in the dead of night… it might be an idea to walk quickly!

WISH YOU WERE HERE?

Stirling

For centuries, nothing has spoken of the great British holiday like the humble postcard. The earliest picture postcard was sent by the English writer Theodore Hook in 1840, and since then the tradition of posting cards to friends and loved ones from holiday destinations has become something of a national pastime. The golden age of the postcard is thought to have been roughly between the years of 1890 and 1915, with many souvenir cards being made available to the public for purchase; a whole industry was soon built up around them.

Stirling has seen many of its famous landmarks used as the subject of postcards over the years, but few have been quite so unusual as Shearer the Stationer's monochrome postcard of the gravestone of Alexander E. Meffen, the first Chief Constable of Stirlingshire. The gravestone itself can still be found at the Valley Cemetery near Stirling Castle. An explanation at the base of the postcard, beneath the main image, explains that the stone's epitaph is attributed to a 1678 quote by Bishop Henshaw of Peterborough reflecting on the brevity of life.

Alexander Meffen was born in Aberdeen around 1821 and started life as a mill worker, before enlisting as a soldier and eventually becoming a member of the Glasgow Police Force. His skill and diligence soon saw him becoming chief detective officer at Dunblane, following which his career advanced rapidly—he was later promoted to chief superintendent and eventually the area's first chief constable. According to historical accounts he was a respected figure, much liked by many of his contemporaries. He died on the 7th of January 1867, never realising that his final resting place would be immortalised in one of Stirling's most eccentric postcards.

JULES VERNE IN SCOTLAND

Aberfoyle

Jules Verne is one of the great pioneers of fantasy and science fiction literature. His masterpieces *Journey to the Centre of the Earth* (1864), *Twenty Thousand Leagues Under the Sea* (1870) and *Around the World in Eighty Days* (1872) are still avidly read and enjoyed even to this very day. What is less widely realised, however, is that this prolific French colossus of adventure writing once penned a novel that took place beneath the charming town of Aberfoyle.

The Child of the Cavern was first published in English in 1877, and is sometimes known by the alternative title *The Underground City*. The novel follows the exploits of mining engineer James Starr, who investigates an abandoned mine near Aberfoyle only to discover that it contains a rich vein of coal... and even has a number of homes within it. A community has developed around the subterranean Loch Malcolm, but a number of unexplained happenings lead Starr to become suspicious. His rational scientific mind unable to accept supernatural explanations, he searches for more earthly causes for threats to the cavern while the mine overman's son explores deep into the caverns and is astonished to find an enigmatic orphaned girl whose presence turns out to be a much more complicated development than it seems. Verne was a notorious stickler for technical accuracy, and the advanced mining project he extrapolates was based on his travels across Scotland and his observations when visiting the coal fields of the River Forth. Many of the advances in tunnelling he suggests would later come to pass, underscoring his famous reputation for technological foresight. While far from Verne's most famous work, the novel has been reissued in new translations in recent years.

A PRECIOUS STONE

Scone

While the Stone of Destiny sounds like a priceless treasure waiting to be unearthed by a bold explorer in a 1980s adventure film, this ancient royal relic actually has its roots near Perth. The Stone of Destiny is a sacred symbol of the monarchy in Scotland, used in the inauguration of ancient kings until John Balliol in 1292. With its earliest origins largely unknown, and theories even speculating Biblical or ninth century links, one thing is certain: thanks to geological testing, we know that the Old Red Sandstone slab was originally quarried in Scone.

However, the Stone of Scone's time in Scotland ended abruptly in 1296 when King Edward I of England seized it. He had it built beneath a new throne at Westminster Abbey for use in the coronation of all the monarchs of England and then Great Britain. All was not lost; although centuries passed, the stone and its heritage were not forgotten. In 1950, four Scottish students reclaimed the stone, removing it from Westminster Abbey and smuggling it back across the border. A countrywide treasure hunt for this historic artefact was underway until it was eventually recovered at Arbroath Abbey.

On St Andrews Day 1996, the stone was officially returned to the people of Scotland, where it was put on display in Edinburgh Castle. Finally, 700 years later, there are plans to return the stone to its rightful home in Perth, Scotland's former capital city. From 2024, the relic is expected to become the centrepiece of Perth City Hall's museum following refurbishment. Fancy starring in your own royal treasure hunt? Take on the Perth Treasure Trail (*www.treasuretrails.co.uk*) to discover the city's hidden gems as you explore its mysteries.

TOWSER THE RECORD-BREAKER

Crieff

The Glenturret Distillery in Crieff (www.theglenturret.com) is considered to be the oldest whisky distillery in Scotland to have always been in continual use. Established in 1775, the distillery still uses its hand-operated mush tun (the only remaining one of its type in Scotland) to hand-craft their single malt whisky, as they have done for more than two centuries. However, the distillery has another claim to fame in that it has been immortalised thanks to a very unexpected Guinness World Record.

From 1963 through to 1987, the distillery's still house was occupied by Towser the cat, a vigilant feline who managed to catch some 28,899 mice in her long and distinguished career on the premises. While cats and distilleries have often been an unfairly overlooked combination—the cat offers its mouse-catching skills in exchange for food and shelter—few have been quite so celebrated as Towser, whose exploits have led to her being almost as synonymous with the Glenturret Distillery as its esteemed product, The Famous Grouse.

Following her death in March 1987, just a few weeks prior to her 24th birthday, Towser was officially recognised as the World's Greatest Mouser, with this title being formally documented by the Guinness Book of Records. It was the very apex of her dedicated service to the distillery, and in tribute there is now a statue of Towser on the grounds which is visited by tourists from all over the world each year. Some have speculated that Towser's amazing success as a mouser came down to the belief that she had a 'tiny wee dram' of whisky in her milk every night, but this dietary supplement is not generally recommended by vets!

BEATRIX POTTER AT BIRNAM

Birnam

Author and illustrator Beatrix Potter remains a hugely well-regarded name in the field of children's literature. Though initially a natural scientist and conservationist who achieved considerable respect in the area of mycology, it was for the publication of her influential book *The Tale of Peter Rabbit* in 1901 that she found worldwide fame. Since her self-publication of the book, it was accepted by Frederick Warne and Company in 1902, was subsequently translated into 36 languages, and has sold in the region of 45 million copies—making it one of the best-selling books of all time.

The Birnam and Dunkeld area greatly inspired Beatrix Potter, who spent her childhood holidays in the region, and her time spent in these picturesque villages is thought to have informed her delightful stories as well as her lifelong interests in the natural sciences. It is thought that she may have gained the creative inspiration for Peter Rabbit (named after a pet rabbit she had owned as a child) and many of her later children's works while holidaying in this area, and certainly when visiting the beautiful parks and woodlands it is easy to see how the spark of imagination may have helped her gentle tales take form.

Situated on Station Road, Birnam, Potter's connection to the village has been commemorated by the establishment of a Beatrix Potter Garden—a landscaped green area which features appearances by many of her beloved characters—as well as a celebrated Beatrix Potter Exhibition at the Birnam Arts Centre (*www.birnamarts.com*) featuring informational displays and many exhibits which celebrate Potter's contribution to children's fiction.

THE FALLS OF BRUAR

Bruar

Of all the the natural features in and around the village of Bruar, none are more striking than the celebrated Falls of Bruar—a beautiful waterfall in forest surroundings which is just a two-mile walk away from the heart of the village. There are two separate walking routes, each leading to two different waterfalls depending on how far visitors want to trek. Most geologists are of the opinion that the falls were formed after the retreat of glaciers from the last Ice Age, at some point during the last 10,000 years; the total drop from the falls is around 60 metres.

The Falls of Bruar only became famous as a tourist attraction at the end of the 18th century, though at that point the surrounding landscape was devoid of trees and thus relatively bleak. Upon visiting the falls, Robert Burns felt compelled to write a short poem, *The Humble Petition of Bruar Water (to the Noble Duke of Athole)*, in 1787, where—in the whimsical guise of the waterfalls themselves—he implored the landowner, the 4th Duke of Atholl, to increase the amount of flora around the area to increase its aesthetic value and make the falls a more attractive location for visitors. In 1796, shortly after Burns had died, the aforementioned Duke—John Murray—finally assented to the request of Scotland's late national bard, and in high style. He ordered some 120,000 Larch and Scots Pine trees to be planted, and arranged for the construction of the two bridges which overlook the falls as well as the path from the village which still remains in use until this day. The result is every bit as impressive as Burns would have hoped, and the forest today includes many genus of trees including Aspen, Willow, Birch and Mountain Ash.

OSSIAN'S HALL

Dunkeld

The Hermitage is a beautiful and peaceful National Trust for Scotland-protected site in Craigvinean Forest along the banks of the River Braan. Considered one of the finest walks in all of Perthshire, the trail takes visitors through an impressive stand of Douglas Firs—among the tallest trees in the United Kingdom—and eventually brings them to the perfect viewing point to observe a very impressive waterfall: the legendary Black Linn Falls of the River Braan.

Originally designed as a pleasure ground for the Dukes of Atholl (who maintained a winter retreat at nearby Dunkeld House) during the eighteenth century, today anyone can enjoy the wonderful sights and sounds of this area. These attraction include Ossian's Hall—a folly constructed in 1757 and rebuilt in 1951, which contains elaborate mirrored panelling and a balcony which boasts incredible views over the Falls.

At one time Ossian's Hall (sometimes known as 'Ossian's Hall of Mirrors') was simply an unimpressive view-house, constructed for the 2nd Duke of Atholl to view the falls from an elevated position. However, in 1783 it was heavily renovated into a shrine for the third century bard Ossian, with mirrors being installed to create the illusion that the waters outside were visible from all angles. The Hermitage was host to many prominent guests over the years, including artist John Turner, composer Felix Mendelssohn and poet William Wordsworth. The building was badly damaged by vandals in 1869 and was left neglected until—many years later, in 1943—the 8th Duchess of Atholl donated it to the National Trust for Scotland, who in 2007 restored it to its original grandeur for everyone to appreciate.

THE WALLACE SWORD

Stirling

The National Wallace Monument in Stirling (*yourstirling.com/see-do/the-wallace-monument*) is undoubtedly one of the most famous sights in the city. Located high upon the hilltop of Abbey Craig, where Sir William Wallace was said to have observed the forces of King Edward I's army assembling prior to the Battle of Stirling Bridge in 1297. The ensuing battle would be one of Scotland's most famous victories, and the monument stands as a commemoration of Wallace and his military prowess.

The monument was designed by John Thomas Rochead and, when completed in 1869, stood at a height of 67 metres (220 feet). Following contributions from the public and overseas donors, it was built from sandstone and remains a hugely popular visitor attraction even today. However, for all its acclaim the building still contains much that may well surprise its guests.

Within its interior, the monument is famous for having a number of artefacts on display which are thought to have belonged to William Wallace, but by far the most celebrated has been the remarkable Wallace Sword—a two-handed longsword measuring 1.63 metres (5 feet and 4 inches) including the hilt, and 2.7 kilograms (5.95 pounds) in weight. This is the sword that is reputed to have been used by Wallace at the Battles of Stirling Bridge and Falkirk, though there has been much historical debate over its authenticity. Why not visit the display and make your own mind up? This must-see exhibit is alone worth climbing the building's 246-step stone spiral staircase in order to view a unique part of Scotland's historical heritage for yourself—just don't forget to enjoy the breathtaking view from the summit when you're there!

IMAGE CREDITS

Page 7: Prisoner of War Artwork at Cultybraggan Camp, near Comrie, is Copyright © Comrie Development Trust, all rights reserved, and is reproduced by kind permission of the copyright holder.

Page 17: Interior of the Thieves' Pot at the Bastion, Stirling, is Copyright © Dr Murray Cook, all rights reserved, and is reproduced by kind permission of the copyright holder.

Page 19: Kinnoull Hill Tower, Perth, is Copyright © Joanne Panton at Shutterstock Inc., all rights reserved, and is reproduced under licence.

Page 23: The Tartan Sheep at Auchingarrich Wildlife Centre, Comrie, is Copyright © Auchingarrich Wildlife Centre, all rights reserved, and is reproduced by kind permission of the copyright holder.

Page 26: Loch Leven Castle, Kinross, by DesignFife at Pixabay. Public domain image.

Page 31: The Bonnety Tree, Stirling, is Copyright © Dr Murray Cook, all rights reserved, and is reproduced by kind permission of the copyright holder.

Page 38: The Hobbit Howf, Braco, is Copyright © Craigend Howfs, all rights reserved, and is reproduced by kind permission of the copyright holder.

Page 41: Cell at the Old Town Jail, Stirling, is Copyright © The Old Town Jail of Stirling, all rights reserved, and is reproduced by kind permission of the copyright holder.

Page 44: The First Haggis in Space is Copyright © Simon Howie Ltd., all rights reserved, and is reproduced by kind permission of the copyright holder.

Page 46: Image of the Fortingall Bell is Copyright © Police Scotland, all rights reserved, and is reproduced by kind permission of the copyright holder.

Page 54: The Secret Chapel, Dunblane, is Copyright © Jenni Barr / Old Churches House Hotel / The Fusion Group, all rights reserved, and is reproduced by kind permission of the copyright holder.

Page 58: Clootie McToot Dumpling is Copyright © Clootie McToot Dumplings, all rights reserved, and is reproduced by kind permission of the copyright holder.

Page 62: Lochhearnhead and Glen Ogle, by Gartnait at Wikimedia Commons. Public domain image.

Page 63: The Deil's Cauldron, Comrie, by Emphyrio at Pixabay. Public domain image.

Page 67: Moirlanich Longhouse, Killin, by Willeangus at Wikimedia Commons. Public domain image.

Page 71: The Monkey Puzzle Tree, by Wikimedia Images at Pixabay. Public domain image.

Page 74: Cairn o' Mohr Winery, Perth, is Copyright © Cairn o' Mohr, all rights reserved, and is reproduced by kind permission of the copyright holder.

Page 75: Red Cap Raspberry Gin Liqueur is Copyright © Stirling Distillery, all rights reserved, and is reproduced by kind permission of the copyright holder.

Page 77: St Adamnán's Standing Stone, Dull, is Copyright © Highland Safaris, all rights reserved, and is reproduced by kind permission of the copyright holder.

Page 79: The Melville Monument, Crieff, is Copyright © alanf at Shutterstock Inc., all rights reserved, and is reproduced under licence.

Page 82: Meikleour Beech Hedge, near Blairgowrie, by MichaelDFowler at Wikimedia Commons. Reproduced under the Creative Commons Attribution-Share Alike 3.0 Unported license. [https://creativecommons.org/licenses/by-sa/3.0/deed.en]

Page 83: The Viaduct Pass of Killiecrankie is Copyright © Ross Pearce at Shutterstock Inc., all rights reserved, and is reproduced under licence.

Page 87: The Western Village, Aberfoyle, is Copyright © Denis Plaxivii at Shutterstock Inc., all rights reserved, and is reproduced under licence.

Page 90: The Stone of Scone, Scone Place, is Copyright © Robert Colonna at Shutterstock Inc., all rights reserved, and is reproduced under licence.

Page 94: Image of Birnam is Copyright © James McDowall at Shutterstock Inc., all rights reserved, and is reproduced under licence.

Page 96: The Falls of Bruar is Copyright © Fabian Junge at Shutterstock Inc., all rights reserved, and is reproduced under licence.

Page 98: Ossian's Hall at Dunkeld is Copyright © PK Perspective at Shutterstock Inc., all rights reserved, and is reproduced under licence.

Page 99: The National Wallace Monument, Stirling, by Sophia Hilmar at Pixabay. Public domain image.

Page 104: Loch Turret by Simon D'Arcy/sidarcy78 at Pixabay. Public domain image.

HEART 200

200 MILES AROUND THE HEART OF SCOTLAND

Heart 200 is a touring route of approximately 200 miles around Perth, Stirling, The Trossachs and Highland Perthshire - the very Heart of Scotland

Discover the beauty and mystery of the Heart of Scotland by following the Heart 200 route. Whatever your personal interests and reasons for wanting to explore Scotland, this route has lots to offer and promises a holiday that will leave you with memories to treasure forever.

www.heart200.scot

 @Heart200Scotland

 @Heart_200_Scotland

ABOUT THE AUTHORS

DR THOMAS CHRISTIE has many years of experience as a literary and publishing professional, working in collaboration with several companies including Cambridge Scholars Publishing, Crescent Moon Publishing, Robert Greene Publishing and Applause Books. A passionate advocate of the written word and literary arts, over the years he has worked to develop original writing for respected organisations such as the Stirling Smith Art Gallery and Museum and a leading independent higher education research unit based at the University of Stirling. Additionally, he is regularly involved in public speaking events and has delivered guest lectures and presentations about his  work at many locations around the United Kingdom. He is co-director of Extremis Publishing, which in September 2021 was named Independent Publishing Company of the Year at the Corporate LiveWire Scotland Prestige Awards.

Tom was elected a Fellow of the Royal Society of Arts in 2018, and is a member of the Royal Society of Literature, the Society of Authors, the Federation of Writers Scotland and the Authors' Licensing and Collecting Society. He holds a first-class Honours degree in English Literature and a Master's degree in Humanities with British Cinema History from the Open University in Milton Keynes, and a Doctorate in Scottish Literature awarded by the University of Stirling.

He is the author of a number of books on the subject of modern film which include *Liv Tyler: Star in Ascendance* (2007), *The Cinema of Richard Linklater* (2008), *John Hughes and Eighties Cinema: Teenage Hopes and American Dreams* (2009), *Ferris Bueller's Day Off: Pocket Movie Guide*

(2010), *The Christmas Movie Book* (2011), *The James Bond Movies of the 1980s* (2013), *Mel Brooks: Genius and Loving It!: Freedom and Liberation in the Cinema of Mel Brooks* (2015), *A Righteously Awesome Eighties Christmas: Festive Cinema of the 1980s* (2016), *John Hughes FAQ* (2019) and *The Golden Age of Christmas Movies: Festive Cinema of the 1940s and 50s* (2019).

His other works include *Notional Identities: Ideology, Genre and National Identity in Popular Scottish Fiction Since the Seventies* (2013), *The Spectrum of Adventure: A Brief History of Interactive Fiction on the Sinclair ZX Spectrum* (2016), *Contested Mindscapes: Exploring Approaches to Dementia in Modern Popular Culture* (2018), and *A Very Spectrum Christmas: Celebrating Seasonal Software on the Sinclair ZX Spectrum* (2021). He has also written a crowdfunded murder-mystery novel, *The Shadow in the Gallery* (2013), which is set during the nineteenth century in Stirling's historic Smith Art Gallery and Museum.

Tom is the author, along with his sister and co-director Julie Christie, of *The Heart 200 Book: A Companion Guide to Scotland's Most Exciting Road Trip* (2020).

For more details about Tom and his work, please visit his website at: www.tomchristiebooks.co.uk

JULIE CHRISTIE has been working in different roles within business and the third sector for more than three decades. Over the years she has worked with a number of charitable organisations such as the Princess Royal Trust for Carers, the Aberlour Childcare Trust, the Alzheimer's Society, the Royal Voluntary Service and Town Break Dementia Care. She was also an associate with the University of Stirling, where she was involved in the development of Dementia Friendly Communities. Julie is currently the Communities and Fundraising Manager for Start Up Stirling, the city's food bank.

She brings considerable experience from the commercial retail industry, having held posts with famous national organisations including AstraZeneca, the NHS, Marks and Spencer, Goldsmiths, Thorntons and Laura Ashley. She holds a Bachelor of Nursing degree from the University of Glasgow and a Bachelor of Science degree with first-class Honours in Sociology and Social Policy from the Open University, which she loved doing as it concentrated on the things that fascinated her about people and culture as well as exploring how we can both see the same thing and yet hold an entirely different point of view.

Her hardest job was dealing with fraught brides when she worked in the wedding trade, where she had to develop her tea-making skills as well as occasionally mopping up tears! The most rewarding job of all – and also the worst-paid – was looking after her late Mum, who had to live with many chronic illnesses.

Julie had never tried being self-employed, so – given her passion for lifelong learning and literacy – the next logical step was to co-found a publishing business, Extremis Publishing Ltd., with her brother Tom. By roping him in to her grand plan, they were able to bring different life skills to the mix. The company specialises in arts, media and culture non-fiction, and their mission is to provide an eclectic range of interesting books, continuing in the long heritage of publishing in the city of Stirling. She is convinced that real life is always more interesting than fiction.

The Heart 200 Book, Julie's first published work, was written in collaboration with her brother and co-director Tom Christie.

Her view on life is that you should never be afraid to try new things, everyone should have a fair chance, that living life is way more interesting than doing the dusting, and that she has never found a box of chocolates that she hasn't liked yet!

Also Available from Extremis Publishing

The Heart 200 Book

A Companion Guide to Scotland's Most Exciting Road Trip

By Thomas A. Christie
and Julie Christie

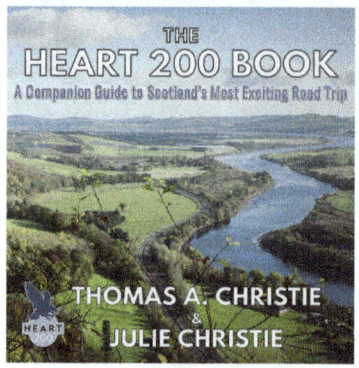

The Heart 200 route is a unique road trip around some of the most beautiful locations in Central Scotland. Two hundred miles running through Stirlingshire and Perthshire, Heart 200 takes its visitors on an epic adventure to suit every taste—whether you are an outdoors enthusiast, an aficionado of history, or simply looking to enjoy yourself in some of the most stunning natural surroundings in the world.

Written with the full approval and co-operation of the Heart 200 team, *The Heart 200 Book* is a guide to the very best that the route has to offer. You will discover the history and culture of this remarkable region, from antiquity to the modern day, with more than a few unexpected insights along the way. Over the millennia, this amazing land has made its mark on world history thanks to famous figures ranging from the ancient Celts and the Roman Empire to King Robert the Bruce and Mary Queen of Scots, by way of Bonnie Prince Charlie, Rob Roy MacGregor, Robert Burns, Sir Walter Scott, Queen Victoria and even The Beatles!

So whether you're travelling by foot, car, motorhome or bike, get ready for a journey like no other as the Heart 200 invites you to encounter standing stones and steamships, castles and chocolatiers, watersports and whisky distilleries... and surprising secrets aplenty! Illustrated with full-colour photography and complete with Internet hyperlinks to accompany the attractions, *The Heart 200 Book* will introduce you to some of the most remarkable places in all of Scotland and encourage you to experience each and every one for yourself. It really will be a tour that you'll never forget.

For details of new and forthcoming books from Extremis Publishing, including our monthly podcasts, please visit our official website at:

www.extremispublishing.com

or follow us on social media at:

www.facebook.com/extremispublishing

www.linkedin.com/company/extremis-publishing-ltd-/

www.ingramcontent.com/pod-product-compliance
Lightning Source LLC
Chambersburg PA
CBHW081416080526
44589CB00016B/2562